The Eighteen Arhat Methods of Shaolin Kungfu

By Cai Longyun
Translated by Huang Long

HAI FENG PUBLISHING COMPANY
Hong Kong   1986

First Edition 1986

Published by
Hai Feng Publishing Co., Ltd.
Rm. 1503 Wing On House,
71 Des Voeux Rd. C., Hong Kong.

Printed by
Friendly Printing Co., Ltd.
Flat B1, 3/F., Luen Ming Hing Ind. Bldg.,
36 Muk Cheong Street, Tokwawan,
Kowloon, H.K.

Distributed by
China International Book Trading Corporation
(GUOJI SHUDIAN)
P.O. Box 399, Beijing, China

Printed in Hong Kong

少林羅漢十八手
蔡龍雲編
黃　龍譯

海峰出版社有限公司出版
（香港德輔道中71號永安集團大廈1503室）

友利印刷有限公司印刷
（香港九龍土瓜灣木廠街36號4樓B1座）

中國國際圖書貿易總公司發行
（中國國際書店）
北京399信箱

1988年（報紙本）第一版
編號：（英文版）
ISBN 962-238-031-X
HF-49-P
T-E-2358P

Contents

Part One:
Applied Tactics of the 18 Methods 1

Part Two:
Arhat Attack-Defence Methods Practised by Two Persons   55

These 18 methods consist of six sets executed with the fist, one set with the elbow, two sets with the palm, four sets with the leg and five sets by catching hold of the opponent. To make successive practice easier, the 18 methods are grouped into a routine of 24 movements. This traditional routine can be practised either by one or two persons. The application of the 18 methods, its applied tactics and the attack-defence methods by two persons are explained in detail as follows:

Part One

Applied Tactics of the 18 Methods

1. THE SINGLE RAFTER (BOW-LEG FIST THRUST)

Movements:
 1. B places right foot to front and left foot at rear (or vice versa) and strikes out right fist to hit at A's left ear (Fig.1).
 2. Swiftly placing left foot to front and right foot at rear, A clenches left fist which he raises up in front of body and swings left to parry B's right fist with wrist (back of A's fist facing upward). He clenches right fist (front of fist facing upward) and draws it to side of waist by bending elbow (Fig. 2a).
 3. Before end of above movement, A twists body left, bends left knee and stretches right leg to form left bow-leg stance. He draws left fist (front of fist facing upward) to side of waist, while thrusting forward right fist (fist front facing floor) to punch B's breast at point where sternum protrudes downward into abdomen. This injures B (Fig. 2b & c).

Essentials:
 1. When the enemy aims at my left ear, he may hit at my temple or the neck artery below the ear, so to ward off the blow with my left fist I should take into consideration the points he aims at by raising my fist higher or lower. But I must use the back of my wrist bone to hit that of the enemy.
 2. When I employ The Single Rafter, I should complete the fist thrust, the stretching of the right leg against the ground behind and the drawing of the left fist to side of waist at the

2a

2b

2c

same time so as to make the leg-stretching move impart, impact and speed to the punch. The aim must be accurate — the lower part of the sternum.

3. If the enemy strikes at my left ear (Fig. 3), I would block his blow with the left fist (Fig. 4a). If the enemy steps backward, I would swiftly step forward with my right foot to close in on him (Fig. 4b). and bend my right knee to land my right fist on the lower part of the enemy's breastbone or sternum. (Fig. 4c & d).

4. If the enemy uses left fist to hit my right ear, I would ward off the blow with my right fist and employ my left fist to execute The Single Rafter against the enemy. This movement can be executed with either the left or right fist.

2. DRAWING THE BOW (HIT OUT ON BENT KNEES)

Movements:
1. A stands with right leg to front and left leg at rear. B steps forward with left foot, places right foot at rear (or vice versa) and swings left fist forward to hit A's right ear, temple or neck artery (Fig. 5).
2. A swiftly clenches right fist and, bending elbow upward, he thrusts fist in rightward curve to ward off B's left fist with that part of his forearm near the wrist where the ulna is (eye of fist facing left). He clenches left fist (front of fist facing upward) and draws it to side of waist (Fig. 6a).
3. With above movement going on, A takes step forward with left leg, turns body right and bends both legs to form horseshoe pattern. Simultaneously, he strikes out left fist from side of waist (front of fist facing floor) to hit at B below the left ribs to injure him (Fig. 6b & c).

Essentials:
1. When Drawing The Bow is executed, the forward thrust of the left fist and the speedy withdrawal of the right arm to the rear should be completed simultaneously as the coordinated movement of the two limbs lends to the blow a more powerful impact.
2. The targets to be hit can be either the kidneys or the spleen, depending on which part of the enemy's body is exposed when he is attacking you.

3. Drawing The Bow may be used on either the left or right side, depending on what tactics the opponent employs.

6a

6b

6c

3. CANNON MOUNTED ON THE BEAM (HIT OUT ON BENT KNEES)

Movements:
  1. B steps forward with right foot (left foot) and sends right fist down on head of A who stands with left foot to front and right foot at rear (Fig. 7).
  2. A acts promptly by clenching left fist (eye of fist facing floor) and raises up left hand in front of him to block B's blow with side of forearm. At same time, he clenches right fist (front of fist facing upward) and withdraws it to side of waist. He leans body a little backward and both his knees are bent (Fig. 8a).
  3. With above movement still going on, A turns body left, stretches right leg and bends left one to form left bow-leg stance. He thrusts right fist (with front of fist facing floor) forward to hit lower part of B's breastbone. This injures B (Fig. 8b & c).

Essentials:
  1. When left forearm with clenched fist is raised to form Cannon Mounted on The Beam to ward off the opponent's strike, one should simultaneously lean his trunk a little backward and bend both knees a little. The backward movement of trunk helps one evade the opponent's blow. When the slightly bent legs are stretched against the ground at the moment the strike is made, they give a more powerful impact to the punch.

7

2. Cannon Mounted on The Beam may be employed on either the left or right side, depending on what tactics the opponent resorts to.

8a

8b

8c

4. THE MONK STRIKES THE BELL (HOLD UP HAND TO DEAL HAMMER BLOW)

Movements:
 1. A stands with left foot to front and right foot at rear. B, stepping forward with right foot (left foot), hammers down right fist at A's head (Fig. 9).
 2. A instantly moves trunk backward to evade blow, swings left arm in upward-downward curve to seize B's right wrist and presses it downward with hand (edge of hand to which thumb attaches facing A). His right arm with clenched fist (front of fist facing floor) is raised in front of him (Fig. 10a).
 3. With above movement still going on, A continues to press down B's right wrist. His right arm moves from behind left arm in upward-forward curve to hit B's forehead with back of fist. He leans trunk toward B and straightens bent right arm. This injures B. (Fig. 10b & c).

Essentials:
 1. The backward dodging of the body, catching hold of opponent's wrist and hitting his head should be executed successively with speed. There should not be the slightest pause in the whole process, otherwise the opponent's left fist may strike while his right wrist is being held.
 2. When the right fist strikes down, attention should be paid not to stiffen the wrist or elbow — the forearm and fist must

be flung out like a whip. The wrist joint, in particular, should be bent upward at the time the right fist is moving upward so that the wrist can be made to flib when the blow is struck.
3. It is best to hit the opponent between the eyebrows.
4. The Monk Strikes The Bell may be employed on either the left or right side, depending on the tactics employed by the opponent.

10a

10b   10c

5. THE DEFT SEWING NEEDLE (HOLD UP ELBOW TO STRIKE)

Movements:
1. B stands with right foot to front and left foot at rear (or vice versa). When A suddenly bends right knee (left knee) to hammer on his head with right fist, B holds up opponent's right arm with left hand (edge of hand to which attaches little finger facing forward) and is ready to strike with right fist (Fig. 11a & b).
2. Before B strikes with right fist after having held up A's arm, A quickly raises left hand (with little finger of hand facing forward) in front of body and holds up B's left hand at the elbow. He simultaneously draws right fist (with front of fist facing upward) to side of waist (Fig. 12a).

11a

11b

12a

3. Before end of above movement, A thrusts right fist (front of fist facing floor) forward to hit B below the ribs. Meanwhile, he clenches left fist (front of fist facing floor) and withdraws it to side of shoulder. B is injured (Fig. 12b & c).

Essentials:
1. In executing The Deft Sewing Needle, the holding up of elbow, withdrawing of fist and striking move should be done in succession simultaneously. Delay in either elbow-holding or striking would give opportunity for the enemy to strike.
2. The upper arm should be held at a point close to the elbow joint to deprive the enemy of the power to press down his arm. No good result can be obtained by holding the enemy's forearm.
3. The right fist strike and the withdrawal of left fist should be executed in coordination simultaneously because the motion of the two limbs lends a greater impact to the thrust of the right fist.

12b

12c

6. SWING THE HAMMER OVER THE BODY (TURNING AROUND TO STRIKE)

Movements:
   1. A stands with right foot to front and left foot at rear. B, who stands behind A, steps forward with right foot (left foot) and shoots right fist on back of A's head (Fig. 13).
   2. A swiftly clenches fist of left hand and swings it behind body (while turning body around from left) in downward-forward-upward curve to strike at B's forearm with side of his own forearm near the wrist joint (eye of fist facing upward) (Fig. 14a).
   3. Before end of above movement, A, utilizing momentum produced by turning around of body, continues to swing right fist up and hammers it down on B's head (fist eye facing upward). Meanwhile he stretches right leg and bends left one to form left bow-leg stance. B is floored (Fig. 14b & c).

Essentials:
   1. In executing the arm swings, the shoulder joints should be kept loose. The arms are swung with great speed to give impetus to the hammering fist blows.
   2. In actual combat, when the trunk is being turned, the right foot must first move a little forward, and the trunk inclines a little to the front so as to evade the enemy's fist blow. Then turn the trunk and swing the arm to strike.

13

3. In actual combat, the enemy may toss his head back to evade your blow. If this happens, hammer on his nose. If the enemy evades the blow by moving his head to the right or left, then strike at his neck or shoulder.

14a

14b

14c

7. THE TWISTED PHEONIX'S ELBOW (BEND KNEE TO BUTT WITH ELBOW)

Movements:

1. A stands with left foot to front and right foot at rear. B steps forward with right foot (left foot) and swings right fist from right side to hit A's left ear (Fig. 15).
2. A swiftly shoots up left arm with clenched fist to parry B's right fist with that part of forearm near wrist. Bending elbow, he draws right fist (fist front facing upward) to side of waist (Fig. 16a).
3. While above movement is in progress, A turns trunk left, bends left knee and stretches right leg to form left bow-leg stance. Simultaneously, he bends right arm and butts B's ribs below right nipple with right elbow (Fig. 16b & c).

Essentials:

1. In doing the elbow butt, attention should be paid to not raising up the shoulder as this would reduce the power of the butt. The shoulder should be kept low.
2. The part to be butted is below the nipple; no good result can be obtained if the elbow thrust lands on the chest above the nipple.
3. The Twisted Phoenix's Elbow is so named because the right elbow butt is made with the left foot in front (or left

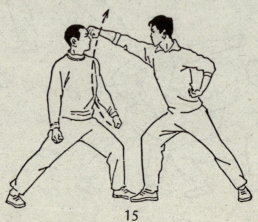

15

elbow butt made with right foot in front) and the foot and elbow are bent. If a right elbow butt is made with the right foot in front and the leg and elbow are not in a twisted posture, then it is called Smooth Phoenix's Elbow.

16a

16b

16c

8. CHOPPING THE LOG (PALM CHOP ON LEG)

Movements:
 1. A stands with left foot to front and right foot at rear. With right foot, B kicks A's crotch or lower abdomen (Fig. 17).

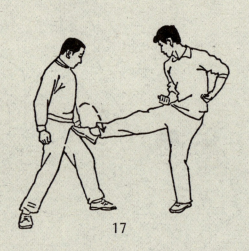
17

 2. A withdraws right foot behind body and turns trunk right to dodge B's kick. At same time, he swings right arm up and, bending elbow, he raises it in leftward curve above head (fingers of palm facing left and edge of palm to which attaches little finger facing upward). He bends elbow to raise left hand in upward-downward curve to chop B's right shin bone (edge of palm to which attaches little finger facing downward, fingers of palm pointing forward and thumb pointing upwards), while bending his legs a little. B is injured (Fig. 18).

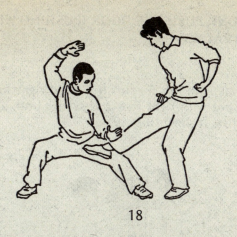

18

Essentials:
1. All these movements — withdrawal of foot, turning of trunk, raising and chopping down of palm should be executed at the same time. There should not be the slightest delay in executing them.
2. The part to be chopped may be the shin bone, the upper part of the foot or tarsal bones, depending on actual conditions existing at the moment.
3. In actual combat, the right hand, as a rule, is not raised. But it must be raised when encountering with a seasoned boxer so as to prevent him from employing The Mandarin Chain Legs. If opponent seeing that your left palm is chopping down, suddenly stretches his left foot against the ground and raises it up to kick at your chin, then you chop down your right palm on his left leg.

9. THE MONK PUSH THE DOOR (PUSHING WITH TWO PALMS)

Movements:
  1. A stands with left foot to front and right foot at rear. B steps forward with right foot and swings both arms to hit A's ears with fists (palms) (Fig. 19).

19

  2. When B's fists are approaching his ears, A raises up right foot from behind by bending knee, thrusts up his hands between B's arms and arches them outward to hit B's wrist bones, thus flinging aside B's fists (palms), (A's fingers facing upward and backs of palms facing forward) (Fig. 20a).
  3. While above movement is going on, A places right foot on floor under B's crotch, bends right knee, stretches left leg and presses both palms against B's breast (Fig. 20b).

20a

20b.

4. Before end of above movement, A stretches both arms to push B to floor (Fig. 20c & d).

20c

20d

Essentials:
  1. In hitting the enemy's wrists with your palms, attention should be paid to keep your elbows close to each other, only turn your forearms outward. The space between the out-turned forearms must not be too big — just a little broader than your shoulders.
  2. In placing your right foot on the floor under the enemy's crotch, your trunk must move foward to close in on the enemy, and with bent elbows, press your palms on the enemy. The enemy can only be pushed down to the floor by simultaneously stretching your left leg against the ground behind and straightening both your arms.
  3. At the moment your body, foot and palms get close to the enemy, you should take advantage of the instant when the enemy tries to withdraw to evade you to stretch your leg and use your arms. This will give the enemy a bad fall.
  4. It is better to place your palms against the ribs of the enemy below the nipples.

10. THE GOLDEN HOOK (HOOK UP THE LEG)

Movements:
 1. A stands with left foot to front and right foot at rear. B steps forward with left foot to strike A's nose or any part of face with left fist (Fig. 21).

21

 2. A swings forward left hand in rightward-upward-leftward direction to grab B's wrist (Fig. 22a).
 3. Before end of above movement, A, shifting foresole of left foot outward and turning body halfway to left, bends knee to lift up right foot from ground behind body, swings up right arm in a curve over his head (fingers of palm pointing backward and front of palm facing left (Fig. 22b).

22a

22b

4. With above movement still going on, A's right leg kicks at B's left calf near the angle bones, hooks up B's left foot and draws it toward his body. (A's foresole pointing upward). Simultaneously he stretches right arm to front of B's breast and with forearm pushes B's body backward (Fig. 22c).

5. With his leg hooked up and body pushed backward, B falls on ground (Fig. 22d).

22c

22d

Essentials:
1. In hooking up enemy's leg, the kicking force of the calf should be used to good advantage, the kicking and upward-hooking moves should be done simultaneously, the momentum generated by the forearm-swing should also be utilized to push the enemy's upper trunk backward — all the moves should be executed with the same speed so as to make The Golden Hook effective.
2. The spot to be hooked must be near the tarsal bones. It should not be too high, otherwise the hooking might move the enemy's body.

11. THE LEG SWEEP (BACKWARD SWEEP IN CROUCHING POSITION)

Movements:

1. A stands with left foot to front and right foot at rear. B steps forward with right foot and punches A's belly with right fist (Fig. 23).

23

2. The moment B's right fist strikes at him, A bends left foot fully, raises left foot's heel from ground, straightens right leg (tiptoe curving upward) along ground, crouches body forward, places straightened arms on floor in front of right foot and, using left sole as pivot, swings arms and twists waist to make right leg sweep backward close to ground to strike B's right foot with that part of his calf that is close to heel. This sweeps B to the floor (Fig. 24a & b).

24a

24b

Essentials:

1. The Leg Sweep derives it power from speed. For this reason, the arm-swinging and body-twisting should be executed suddenly with great force at the moment of body-crouching. The outward turning of the left heel should also coordinate with waist-twisting and arm-swinging.
2. The right foot should be made to touch the ground when it is swept back, but it is not to be pressed against the floor too heavily. The angle between the right leg and the trunk must be below 90 degrees throughout the execution of The Leg Sweep.
3. In doing The Leg Sweep, you should crouch and sweep back your leg swiftly whether the enemy aims at your abdomen or face the instant the enemy starts stepping forward to mount a frontal attack. Do not wait until his blows come close to your body as shown in Fig. 23.

12. THE BALL KICK (KICK WITH ONE FOOT)

Movements:
When he is confronted with any frontal attacks by B, A should kick out right leg (left leg) at B's calf, crotch or lower abdomen (instep stretched tight, tiptoe pointing forward) (Fig. 25).

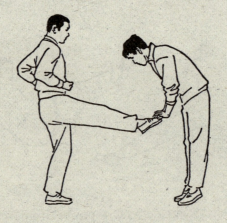

25

Essentials:
1. Before making the kick, the calf should be raised above the ground behind the body by bending the knee, and stretch tight the instep with the toes bending downward. Then kick with speed like one kicking a ball. The forward kick is not executed from behind the body with a straightened leg, and the raising of the calf and the forward kick are to be done together simultaneously, not separately.
2. The kick must not be too high, and when aiming at the enemy's calf, the left leg supporting the weight of the body must be kept a little bent at the knee.

13. THE MANDARIN DUCK FEET (DOUBLE KICKS)

Movements:
1. No matter what frontal attacks B mounts against A, the latter can kick out left foot (with toes pointing forward and instep stretched tight) at B's lower abdomen or crotch (Fig. 26a).

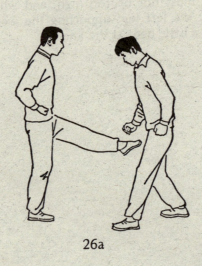

26a

2. With above movement still going on, B draws in abdomen to evade A's left-foot kick (Fig. 26b). Then A's right foot (instep stretched taut) springs up from ground to kick B's chin with tiptoe. B is injured. When his right foot kicks up, A's left foot is lowered to floor (Fig. 26c).

Essentials:
1. In The Mandarin Duck Feet method, the left-foot kick is, in general, something "vague" to lure the enemy to evade the

strike by drawing in his abdomen, and in so doing bends forward his upper trunk. Then the right foot kicks — this is the "real" thing. However, there is in Wushu what is real in what is vague. The "vague" kick of the left foot can be converted into a "real" one if the enemy is slow in evading the kick.

2. The springing up of the right foot and the lowering of the left one must be executed simultaneously, because the upward and downward movements of the two limbs go together to give a great force to the right-foot kick.

26b

26c

14. THE EAGLE SEIZES THE GULLET (GRIPPING THROUGH WITH HAND)

Movements:
 1. A stands with left foot to front and right foot to rear. B steps forward with right foot (left foot) to punch A's breast with right fist (Fig. 27).

27

 2. Raising up left hand in front of him and swinging it in rightward-upward-leftward curve, A seizes B's right wrist (front of hand facing floor, thumb pointing forward). Then A turns forearm outward (to make front of hand facing upward) to twist B's forearm outward (Fig. 28a).
 3. Before above movement ends, as he is twisting B's right wrist outward, A steps forward with right foot and his right hand at side of waist stretches out to seize B's throat between thumb and fingers (front of palm facing floor) (Fig. 28b).

28a

28b

Essentials:

1. If your aim is to push down the enemy in executing The Eagle Seizes The Gullet, then loose your hold on the enemy's wrist to let him fall backward at moment you seize his throat. If the aim is to choke him, then don't let go his wrist, but grasp his throat firmly with your thumb and fingers.

2. The spot of the throat to be clutched should be between the Adam's apple and the cartilage of the tongue. This will stop the intake of air in the wind-pipe. When the thumb and fingers are squeezed together, they should be pressed against the left and right arteries in the neck to stop the flow of blood to the brain.

15. CARRY THE BASKET ON THE ARM (HOOK UP ARM WITH ELBOW)

Movements:
1. A stands with left foot to front and right foot at rear. B takes step forward with right foot (left foot) to strike A's breast with right fist. (Fig. 29).

29

2. A moves left hand up from under B's right fist and sends it in rightward-upward-leftward curve to grasp B's right wrist (front of hand facing floor, edge of hand to which attaches thumb facing forward) (Fig. 30a).
3. Before above movement ends, A, while holding B's right wrist, turns forearm outward (with front of hand facing upward) to twist B's right arm outward. Simultaneously, A strides forward with right foot while turning trunk left, and, passing right arm with clenched fist under B's right arm, he curves it up in front of him. Then, bending elbow to hook B's arm at the elbow, he jerks up right arm with force, while his left hand, which grasps B's right wrist, presses downward with force. B's right arm elbow is jerked and pressed upward and downward at same time (Fig. 30b).

30a

30b

4. After having held up B's right arm, A turns right fist into palm and swings it to chop B's back where kidneys are (front of palm facing floor) (Fig. 30c). B instantly falls to ground with injury to elbow and kidneys (Fig. 30d).

30c

30d

Essentials:
1. The holding up of the arm should be done swiftly. The hooking up of the right elbow and the pressing by the left hand should be executed with force in a split second.
2. The holding up of the arm should not be done in a stereotyped manner. If the enemy finds out your intention and raises up his elbow to make it impossible for you to hold up his arm, don't execute the arm holding move foolhardily. Then chop on his back where the kidneys are. This can also be effective if properly done.
3. The secret to the success in holding up arm in Carry The Basket on the Arm is seizing the wrist and twisting the limb. When you have got hold of the wrist, you should grasp it firmly and swiftly twist the arm outward to make it impossible for the enemy to bend his elbow and raise up his arm before the twisting begins. If the enemy bends his elbow and raises his arm in a split second after the twisting begins to make it impossible for you to hook and push up his arm at the elbow, you should press the forearm of your bent arm against the outer edge of the enemy's elbow to push it in an upward direction, while your left arm, which grasps the enemy's wrist is pushed down in an outward direction, thus changing the upward-downward movement into an inward-outward one. This can also achieve good result in arm holding.

16. TWISTING THE STRAND OF SILK (TWIST ARM TO INJURE WRIST)

Movements:
1. B steps forward with right foot (left foot) to grab at A's breast with right hand (Fig. 31).

31

2. A's right hand curves upward to block B's right hand with that part of forearm close to wrist. He wards off B's breast-grabbing hand and lets him catch hold of his forearm at the wrist (Fig. 32a).
3. While above mevement is in progress, A swiftly places left hand on back of B's right hand and holds it firmly (front of A's hand facing floor) with thumb firmly grasping B's four fingers, and his four fingers are pressed together to get a firm grip on B's hand at spot where the thumb and fingers meet. A's hand firmly pressed against back of B's right hand. A simultaneously sticks out thumb of right hand whose fingers are pressed together and curves up right palm (fingers pointing upward) (Fig.32b).

32a

32b

4. Before above movement ends, A's left hand graps B's right hand firmly. He cuts B's wrist with side of right palm to which attaches little finger, and he follows up by executing outward-downward-inward twisting move followed by turning his right arm sideways. This injures B's wrist (Fig. 32c).

Essentials:
1. In executing Twisting The Strand of Silk, you should get hold of enemy's hand that grabs your arm with one hand, and use the palm of the other hand to cut (with edge of palm to which little finger attaches) on the spot of the enemy's arm where the ulna and carpal bones meet, and twist to injure the tendons and tissues of his wrist. This will dislocate the wrist joint when done with force.
2. When employing the twisting method, you should utilize the momentum of the pull with which the enemy's hand drags your forearm toward him, and hold his hand firmly to draw it toward your body. The dragging and drawing motions will help loosen the enemy's wrist joint to make it easier for the edge of your palm to cut in.
3. As the upward movement of your right arm to parry the enemy's breast-grabbing hand is a ruse to lure him into getting hold of your forearm, you should only raise up your right hand just at the moment his hand is about to grab your breast, thus making him to catch hold of your forearm and not your breast.

32c

17. THE DRAGON-SUBDUCING HAND (GRASP ELBOW TO CUT WRIST)

Movements:
1. B moves forward with left foot (right foot) and twists left arm inward (thumb facing floor) to seize A's forearm near wrist in preparation to mount attack on A. (Fig. 33).

33

2. A swiftly raises up right arm by bending elbow, and clenches right fist (front of fist facing floor); his left arm comes up to lay on back of B's left hand and grasps it firmly. His thumb firmly holding fingers of B's left hand, while his fingers are pressed together to get firm hold on edge of B's left hand to which attaches little finger (Fig. 34a).
3. While above movement is in progress, A's left hand swiftly grips B's left hand firmly, and his right forearm, which presses on B's left wrist, twists in upward-inward-forward-downward direction, and his body moves forward and downward simultaneously. Injured, B falls (Fig. 34b).

34a

34b

Essentials:
Both the elbow-folding and hand-twisting are catching moves executed to cut wrist and to injure and dislocate the enemy's wrist joint. In the two hand-twisting moves, the edge of the palm is used to cut the enemy's wrist when the twisting is proceeding; and in the elbow-folding move the forearm is used to press firmly the enemy's wrist joint while the folding is taking place. In both cases, the enemy's wrist is twisted in spiral manner. Wrist-cutting would be ineffective by pressing on the enemy's wrist alone.

18. THE MONK ROPES THE TIGER (PRESS DOWN ELBOW TO FOLD WRIST)

Movements:

1. B strides forward with right foot (left foot) to lay hold on A's left shoulder with right hand. (Fig. 35).

35

2. A swiftly swings up right hand to grip B's right hand (A's thumb firmly pressing on B's right hand fingers while his fingers firmly grasping edge of B's hand to which attaches little finger). A simultaneously moves trunk backward to drag B's right hand toward him (Fig. 36a).

3. Before above movement ends, A promptly turns body right, lowers right elbow and with right hand grips B's right hand and drags it toward him while twisting it downward. At same time, his left hand with clenched fist goes up in a curve to bring elbow above B's right arm (front of fist facing backward) (Fig. 36b).

36a

36b

4. With above movement going on, A continues to lower his left elbow and to press upon B's right wrist with upper arm, while bending both knees and twisting trunk left. His left upper arm presses B's right wrist downward and forward in a twisting move to injure B's wrist (Fig. 36c).

5. After injuring B's wrist, A turns left fist into palm and sends it right to pass by right shoulder in forward-leftward curve to chop right side of B's breast with edge of palm to which attaches little finger. This floors B (Fig. 36d & e).

Essentials:

The gist of pushing down elbow to cut wrist in The Monk Ropes The Tiger is twisting. The bending of both the knees to shift down body weight is to increase the pressure on the opponent's wrist. The turning of the body left is meant to enhance the pressing and twisting power of the left upper arm. Hence, the bending of knees and downward shift of body weight should coordinate with the move to press down the elbow. The body-turning move should also coordinate with the twisting move of the upper arm.

36c

36d

36e

Part Two

Arhat Attack-Defence Methods
Practised by Two Persons

PREPARATORY MOVES

1. A and B stand at attention.

Movements:
A and B stand side by side with four or six paces between them, A facing south and B facing north (Fig. 1).

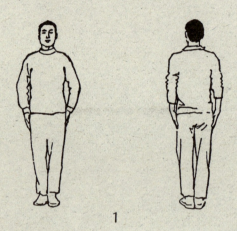

1

Essentials:
Head is held upright, chin drawn in, chest help up, waist straightened, shoulders kept low and elbows bent slightly naturally and raised a little infront of body. Be calm mentally and keep worldly cares out of mind to concentrate thoughts on direction fist is to thrust and be ready to strike.

2. A and B Clench Their Fists.

Movements:
Both place fists beside their waists by bending elbows (with front of fist facing upward) and turn faces left with eyes on each other (Fig. 2).

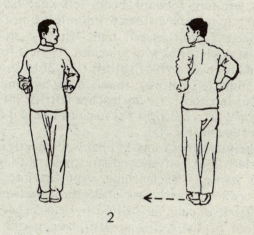

2

Essentials:
1. Fist-clenching and face-turning should be done quickly and simultaneously.
2. Body inclined little forward with weight on feet and toes pressed against floor. Take care not to bend waist and hunch back. Press bent elbows against body with elbows pointing backward.

SECTION ONE

1. **B Punches A's Ribs With Fist.**
   A Retaliates With The Eagle Seizes The Gullet.

Movements:
   1. B turns tiptoe of left foot sideways, twists trunk left and steps forward with right foot (Fig. 3a).
   2. B moves left foot forward, bends left knee halfway and stretches right foot against floor to form left bow-leg stance. He simultaneously punches out right fist (fist front facing floor) to hit at A's left ribs with knuckles. His left fist remains where it is and his eyes on his right fist (Fig. 3b).
   3. A turns trunk left halfway, lowers body by bending knees and moves out left foot. He unclenches left fist into palm to grasp B's right wrist. His right fist remains where it is, and his eyes on his left palm (Fig. 4a).
   4. Immediately twisting trunk left halfway once again to face B, A bends left knee halfway and stretches right leg to form left bow-leg stance. Unclenching right fist into palm, he stretches it forward to catch hold of B's throat between thumb and fingers (front of palm facing floor). He clenches left palm into fist (front of fist facing upward) and places it beside waist. His eyes on his right palm (Fig. 4b).

Essentials:
When punching A's ribs, B should execute the fist-striking and knee-bending moves with the same speed. The part to be hit must be the side of A's breast below the nipple. But in practice exercise, the fist is to be extended only close to A's body and never to touch it to avoid inflicting injury to him. The seizing of the throat must not be executed as in a real fight, just pat B's chest below the throat with centre of the palm (thumb and fingers pointing upwards).

2. B Holds Up A's Arm, A Does The Same To Him.

Movements:
   1. Unclenching left fist into palm and forming fork with thumb and fingers, B swings left arm in inward-upward direction to hold up A's right forearm, thus preventing opponent from seizing his throat. He bends elbow to draw right fist (front of fist facing upward) beside waist. His eyes on his left palm (Fig. 5).
   2. Swiftly unclenching left fist into palm and forming fork with thumb and fingers, A swings left arm in inward-forward-upward curve to hold up B's left arm, thus preventing B from holding up his own arm. His eyes on his left palm (Fig. 6a).
   3. Both A and B shift weight of body backward, bend their right knees halfway and draw left feet half a step to touch floor with tiptoes by bending knees. Both press thumbs and fingers of left palms together (thumbs and fingers pointing upward, edges of palms to which attach little fingers facing forward) and hold up palms in front of bodies. Trunks of both are twisted halfway to right. B still clenches right fist, while A draws right palm (fingers pointing floor and front of palm facing forward) to side of waist. Both eye each other (Fig. 6b).

Essentials:
   In actual combat, the arm-holding move should be executed the moment the enemy's outstretched hand is about to touch you. It should not be done earlier or later. If executed too early, the enemy might withdraw his hand, and if done too late, the enemy's move might have succeeded. In a practice exercise, you may let your opponent complete his move and then hold up his arm so as to gain a better understanding of the method.

3. **B Punches A's Face,
Latter Retaliates With Carrying The Basket On The Arm**

Movements:
   1. Shifting weight of body forward, B steps forward with right foot, bends right knee halfway and stretches left leg against ground to form right bow-leg stance. He folds left palm into fist and draws it to side of waist (front of fist facing floor). He thrusts forward right fist which passes by outward edge of A's left palm to hit A's face (front of fist facing floor) (Fig. 7).

7

   2. A steps forward with left leg and swings left palm in downward-inward-outward curve with elbow joint acting as hinge. He grasps B's right wrist. His eyes on his left palm (Fig. 8a).
   3. Before end of above movement, A takes big stride forward with right foot, turns body left to face north and bends both knees half-way to form horse-shoe pattern. He turns left arm leftward to twist round B's right arm (front of A's fist facing floor). A folds right palm into fist, which moves downward from side of waist, passes in front of his body, goes under B's right arm and rises upward as A bends elbow (eye of fist facing right). A presses down left hand and pushes up right elbow with force to break B's elbow. His eyes on B (Fig. 8b, front and back views).

8a

8b-front view

8b-back view

Essentials:
  When making the big stride forward, A should see that his right foot is placed near inward side of B's right foot. The elbow-breaking move should not be overdone, just execute it in a token manner. In hitting A's face, B should only strike his right fist just to front of A's nose, never to touch A's face.

4. B Chops A's Skull With Palm, Latter Does Drawing The Bow

Movements:

 1. B unclenches left fist into palm and swings it up from side of waist in downward-leftward-forward curve to chop behind A's right ear with edge of palm to which attaches little finger (front of palm facing upward). His eyes on his left palm (Fig. 9).

9

 2. A pulls back right fist from below B's right arm and swings it up to parry B's left palm. Letting go his left-hand grip on B's right wrist, A bends elbow to draw left fist (front of fist facing upward) beside waist. His eyes on his right fist. B then draws right fist (front of fist facing upward) to side of waist (Fig. 10a).

 3. Before above movement ends, A gyrates left tiptoe sideways and turns trunk right to effect about turn, while his left foot takes big strike to east. He strikes left fist forward to hit B's breast or belly with knuckles. B simultaneously steps back with right foot (Fig. 10b).

10a

10b

4. With above movement still going on, A, whose body is facing south, bends both knees halfway to form horse-shoe pattern. He bends elbow to curve right hand upward and shoots out left fist (front of fist facing floor). B simultaneously stretches left leg, bends right one, twists trunk rightward to face north and leans body right to dodge A's left fist strike. He follows up by raising left palm and twists arm inward to bend wrist to make front of palm face upward. His eyes on A's left fist (Fig. 10c).

10c

Essentials:

The three moves of A — parrying with right fist, the big stride made by left foot and the left fist punch — should be executed in succession. B's withdrawal of foot and dodging should be executed with the raising of palm and the bending of body the moment A's left fist thrusts forward. He should not dodge too late. A and B should execute the moves in close coordination. A should thrust out his fist just at the moment B bends body — neither too early nor too fast. The bending of B's body is not to be done too slowly or too early. He should withdraw his foot just at the moment A steps forward, and bends his body the moment A strikes out his fist.

5. B Chops A's Head With Palm, Latter Reacts With Cannon Mounted On The Beam

Movements:
1. B stretches right leg, bends left knee and flings downward left palm (with thumb sticking out and fork formed between thumb and index finger facing forward) to beat on back of A's left fist. At same time, he moves right fist from side of waist in downward-rightward-upward curve and twists arm outward to make knuckles of fist face upward in slanting manner. His eyes on A's head. At this instant, A bends elbow to draw right fist (front of fist facing upward) to side of waist (Fig. 11a).
2. Before end of above movement, B turns trunk left and chops A's head with right fist (eye of fist facing upward). He clenches left palm into fist and draws it to side of waist (front of fist facing upward). His eyes on his right fist (Fig. 11b).
3. A bends elbow to raise left hand with clenched fist (eye of fist facing floor) to hold up B's right fist with forearm. His eyes on B's right fist (Fig. 12a).
4. Before above movement ends, A twists trunk left, bends left knee halfway and stretches right leg against ground to from left bow-leg stance. A simultaneously thrusts forward right fist (front of fist facing floor) to hit B's breast or belly. His eyes fix on his right fist (Fig. 12b).

11a

Essentials:
The beating down of B's left palm and his right-fist chop should be executed together to form a perfect movement with no delay in between. So should the raising up of A's left fist and the thrusting out of his right fist. But care should be taken not to touch B's body when the fist thrusts forward.

6. B holds A's wrist,
A Does The Dragon-Subduing Hand

Movements:

1. B unfolds left fist into palm, swings left arm from side of waist in leftward-upward-rightward-downward curve to grab A's right wrist with his palm (edge of palm to which attaches little finger facing forward). His eyes on his left palm (Fig. 13).

13

2. A turns left fist into palm which moves down to catch hold of B's left palm (edge of A's palm to which attaches little finger facing forward). His eyes on his left palm. B simultaneously draws right fist (front of fist facing upward) to side of waist (Fig. 14a).

3. While above movement is still in progress, A immediately pulls back left foot half a step, moves right foot forward and twists trunk left. Using right fist and left palm, A drags B's left hand toward right side of his breast. Simultaneously, he presses firmly on B's left wrist with right forearm which, starting from side of B's left arm, twists in upward-inward-forward-downward direction. He stretches left leg against ground, bends right knee to form right bow-leg stance and casts eyes on B. This compells B to stretch left arm and left leg and bend right knee. With body inclined forward, B turns back head to stare at A (Fig. 14b, front and back views).

Essentials:

In executing elbow-folding and wrist-cutting move in a practice exercise, A should never uses his forearm to press hard on

B's wrist and wind it in outward-inward direction. His forearm can only be pressed on the back on B's elbow in such a way so as to make him feel no pressure on his wrist. B should twist his forearm inward and stretch his arm. A's right foot should be placed outside B's left foot.

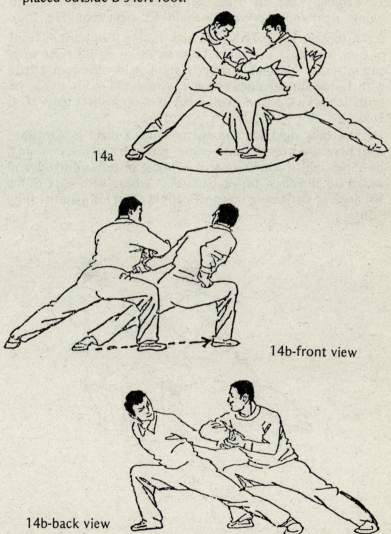

14a

14b-front view

14b-back view

7. B Swings Body Around To Hit, A Counters With The Monk Strikes The Bell.

Movements:
   1. Bending knee to draw left foot close to right one, B swings right foot backward behind A's right foot (Fig. 15a).

   2. A loosens left palm's hold and, raising it upward in front of him, swings it backward to come down on B's right wrist and seizes it. He simultaneously straightens right foot a little with tiptoe turned sideways and, straightening his trunk, he turns it backward from right. His eyes on his left palm (Fig. 16a).

He stretches right leg and twists trunk around in rightward direction, and with the momentum generated by body-turning, he flings right hand from side of waist in forward-rightward-backward direction to hit back of A's head with back of his fist (eye of fist facing upward). His eyes on his right fist (Fig. 15b).

15a

15b

16a

3. Before end of above movement, when A is twisting trunk around to grasp his wrist, B loosens his left hand's hold on A's right fist and clenches left fist which he draws to side of waist (front of fist facing upward). B immediately twists trunk backward from right to face north. He takes big stride with left foot to left side of his body, moves right foot a step to right side and bends both knees halfway to form horse-shoe pattern. At moment B turns body and bends knees, A twists body backward to face south and making big step to left side of body with left foot and half step to right side of body with right foot; he bends both knees halfway to form horse-shoe pattern. He bends elbow to raise up right fist which, after moving up in front of his face, hammers at B's forehead as A straightens his elbow. His eyes on his right fist (Fig. 16b, front and side views).

Essentials:
In these movements, both A and B execute body-twisting and feet-exchanging moves at the same time. By feet exchanging, it means that the left and right feet exchange positions — the left foot shifts close to the right foot at the moment of body-twisting while the right foot shifts to where the left foot was after body-turning move. To effect close coordination between the two partners, A, while exchanging feet, has to take into account B's moves — he should adjust the width created by his striding and shifting feet to the distance between B's bent feet and places them just in front of B's feet. A's blow on B's forehead should be executed the instant B turns his body and bends his knees. No delay is permitted because any delay would prevent B from striking out his left fist, thus undermining the standard and solemnity of the practice exercise.

16b-front view

16b-side view

8. B Bends Knee and Hold Up A's Elbow, A Counters With The Deft Sewing Needle

Movements:
  1. Immediately follwong above movement, B unclenches left fist into palm (with thumb separated from fingers) and raises up arm to hold up A's right arm at elbow with palm. His eyes on his left palm (Fig. 17).

  2. A, swiftly sticking out thumb of left palm, raises left hand in front of him to hold up B's left arm at elbow with palm. He draws right fist (front of fist facing floor) to side of waist. His eyes on his left palm. At same moment, B also draws his right fist (front of fist facing upward) to side of waist (Fig. 18a, front and side views).
  3. Before above movement ends, A thrusts forward right fist (front of fist facing floor) at B's breast to hit it with knuckles. His eyes on his right fist (Fig. 18b, front and side views).

Essentials:
  In holding each other's arm, A and B should not raise up their shoulders, and their bent knees should remain as they are when they hold up each other's elbow and strike out fists.

18a-front view

18a-side view

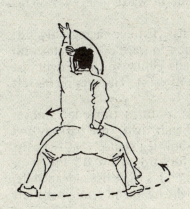

18b-front view

18b-side view

9. B Does Hand-Chop,
A Executes The Single Rafter

Movements:
1. Following above movement, A, after thrusting out right fist, swiftly clenches left palm into fist (front of fist facing upward) and withdraws it to side of waist. B bends elbow to raise left palm and flings it in rightward-downward-leftward curve to ward off A's right fist. He simultaneously straightens both legs, and his left foot steps sideways to outward edge of A's left foot (B's left foot's tiptoe gyrating sideways). His eyes on his left palm (Fig. 19a).
2. Before above movements ends, B follows up by swinging right foot in wide arch to east and twisting trunk left to face west. He bends left knee halfway and straightens right leg to form left bow-leg stance. He unfolds right fist into palm and swings it from side of waist in downward-backward-rightward-forward curve to chop on back of A's head with edge of palm (front of palm facing floor) to which attaches little finger. At same moment, he clenches left palm into fist (front of fist facing upward) and draws it to side of waist. His eyes on his right palm (Fig. 19b).
3. A bends elbow to raise left fist (fist eye facing outward) and flings it up in outward direction to ward off B's palm with forearm. He simultaneously bends elbow to draw right fist (fist front facing upward) to side of waist. His eyes on his left fist (Fig. 20a).
4. Before above movement ends, A turns trunk left, moves forward to east with right foot, bends right knee halfway and straightens left leg to form right bow-leg stance. His right fist (fist front facing floor) strikes forward to hit B's breast or abdomen with knuckles. His eyes on his right fist. Meanwhile, B draws left foot back, bends right knee and straightens left leg (Fig. 20b)

Essentials:
Here B does a big foot swing. In doing so, he should move his left foot in a curve from left to right to pass his right foot in an outward direction to bring it to the outward edge of A's left foot. The oblique move of his right foot should also take

the form of a curve. B's hand-chopping strike and flinging out of left palm should begin the moment he starts swinging his left foot. His right-palm chop should begin the moment he starts swinging his right foot. The moves should be executed in succession and coordination.

10 B Does Sideways Hand Chop, A Counters With The Single Rafter

Movements:
1. Following preceeding movement, A, after striking out right fist, swiftly draws left fist (fist front facing upward) to side of waist. B bends elbow to send right palm in leftward-downward-rightward curve to push aside A's right fist. His eyes on his right palm (Fig. 21a).

21a

2. Before above movement ends, B unfolds left fist into palm which he swings from side of waist in downward-backward-leftward-forward curve to chop above A's right ear with edge of palm to which attaches little finger (front of palm facing upward). He instantaneously turns right palm into fist (front of fist facing upward) and draws it to side of waist. His eyes on his left palm (Fig. 21b).
3. Bending elbow to raise right fist, A flings right forearm in outward direction to block B's left palm. His eyes on his right fist (Fig. 22a).
4. Before end of above movement, A turns trunk right, steps forward with left foot, bends left knee and stretches right leg against ground to form left bow-leg stance. He jabs forward left fist (fist front facing floor) to hit B's abdomen with knuckles. His eyes on his left fist. B simultaneously moves right foot back, bends left knee and stretches right leg against ground (Fig. 22b).

Essentials:

After swinging out right hand to parry A's right fist, B should not hold straight his right arm but withdraws it to his waist. When A strikes out fist, he should take care of personal safety by stepping forward first, and punches out his fist only after B has pulled back right foot.

21b

22a

22b

11. B Executes Palm-Chopping And Fist Punch, A Does The Golden Hook

Movements:
1. Continuing preceeding movement, A, after delivering left fist punch, swiftly draws to side of waist right fist (front of fist facing upward). B bends elbow to lower left palm which, moving to right side of breast, goes in downward-leftward curve to ward off A's left fist. His eyes on his left palm (Fig. 23a).
2. Before above movement ends, B unfolds right fist into palm and moves it from side of waist in downward-backward-rightward-forward curve to chop on A's left ear (with edge of palm to which attaches little finger and with front of palm facing upward). Meanwhile, he turns left palm into fist (fist front facing upward) and draws it to left side of waist. His eyes on his right palm (Fig. 23b).

3. A bends elbow to raise left fist and flings left forearm sideways to block B's right palm. His eyes on his left fist (Fig. 24).
4. At moment his palm is blocked by A's left fist, B strikes forward left fist (fist front facing floor) to punch at A's chin. His eyes on his left fist (Fig. 25).

23a

23b

24

25

5. Turning left fist into palm, A swings it downward to pass his face to grip B's left wrist (edge of palm to which attaches little finger facing forward). B simultaneously clenches right palm into fist (front of fist facing upward) which he draws to side of waist (Fig. 26a).

6. Before above movement ends, A immediately stands on left leg (knee still bending a little). Unfolding right fist into palm, he bends elbow to fling forearm in rightward-upward direction to pass by right ear and thrusts it forward over B's left arm as he straightens arm to jap it at B's breast (face of palm facing floor, and A's elbow is a little bent). He simultaneously bends knee to lift right foot (tiptoe pointing downward) from ground behind body. His eyes on his right palm (Fig. 26b).

7. With above movement still in progress, A kicks out right foot to hook heel of B's left leg. B swiftly raises left foot to dodge A's hooking kick (Fig. 26c).

Essentials:

B should swiftly punch at A's chin with left fist the moment the latter does his parrying move so as not to let his opponent execute The Single Rafter as he has done on two occasions previously. He delivers the punch before his opponent strikes out his fist. A's holding of opponent's hand, stretching out of palm and hooking kick should be executed swiftly and in succession. But in doing the hooking kick, he is not to fling B sideways with right palm as in actual combat; his right-foot hooking kick should be executed when B is about to bend his knee and lift his foot. Do not hook up the heel as in actual combat. Both partners should act in strict coordination.

26a

26b

26c

12. B Grabs A's Breast With Palm, A Executes Twisting The Strand Of Silk

Movements:
   1. Following preceeding move, A's left palm lets go B's left wrist, and he moves left arm in downward-leftward curve to hold it horizontally with elbow slightly bent (fingers of palm pointing upward and front of palm facing forward). He swings right palm in downward-rightward curve and holds right arm horizontally (with fingers of hand facing floor). He kicks out right foot obliquely in northeast direction (tiptoe pointing upward). His eyes on B. B simultaneously withdraws left leg in northerly direction and straightens it. He bends right knee to form right bow-leg stance and draws left fist (front of fist facing upward) to side of waist. Unfolding right fist into palm (thumb separated from fingers which point upward), he thrusts right arm forward with intention of grabbing A's breast. His eyes on A's breast (Fig. 27).

27

2. The moment B grabs at his breast, A turns curved right hand into palm and swings it down toward body and raises it up as he bends elbow (front of palm facing floor); and he intercepts B's breast-grabbing hand with that part of right forearm near wrist, thus B's breast-grabbing effort is foiled and wrist of his right hand is caught by A. A bends elbow to make left palm lay firm grip on B's right hand. He simultaneously lifts right leg in front of body by bending knee. His eyes on his right palm (Fig. 28a).

28a

3. Before end of above movement, A cuts B's wrist with edge of right palm (to which attaches little finger) by moving it in upward-outward-downward-inward manner, while turning right arm sideways. He twists trunk right, bends right knee slightly and lifts left foot above floor by bending knee. His eyes on his right palm. (Fig. 28b).

4. Before end of above movement, A twists trunk to face south and, placing left foot on floor on outward side of B's right foot, he bends both knees to form horse-shoe pattern. Meanwhile, he turns left palm into fist which strikes at B's nose; his right palm which loosens hold on B's right hand is clenched into fist (front of fist facing upward) and withdrawn to side of waist. His eyes on B's face (Fig. 29).

28b

29

Essentials:
In practice exercise, A should never twist and cut B's wrist as in actual combat; he should just catch hold of B's wrist with his right hand and give it a slight outward twist. His left hand should not lay a firm hold on B's right hand. In the nose-striking punch, care should be taken not to touch B physically.

13. B Parries Blow With Palm, A Does The Leg Sweep

Movements:
1. Drawing right leg behind body and stretching it, B bends left knee to form left bow-leg stance. He simultaneously unclenches left fist into palm which, moving forward from side of waist, passes under A's left fist and parries it (fingers of palm pointing upward and edge of palm to which little finger attaches facing forward). Turning right palm into fist (front of fist facing upward), he draws it to side of waist. His eyes on his left palm (Fig. 30).
2. Gyrating sole of left foot sideways and bending left leg fully, A stretches out right leg which sweeps backward at B as A bends body to right and twists waist. B, instantaneously raising right foot and stretching left foot against ground, leaps over A's right leg to west, thus dodging A's leg sweep (Fig. 31).
3. Landing on right leg, B twists trunk left to face south and lifts up left foot (instep stretched taut and tiptoe pointing floor obliquely). He simultaneously turns right fist into palm (front of palm facing upward) which is flung up rightward (fingers pointing rightward). He draws left palm (front of palm facing upward) and positions it below right armpit. His eyes on his right palm (Fig. 32).

Essentials:
In executing the backward leg sweep, A should straighten his right leg and sweeps it along the ground. When B leaps, he should jump farther and land lightly and steadily. When lifting his left foot, he should position it before his right knee with the calf slanting downward. In raising up his palm, he should place it level to the shoulders. In bending his left elbow, he should keep it close to his body. In practice by two persons, the leaping is a "pass the door" move which means that when one move is completed and the other begins, both partners are to change positions. In doing this both partners should coordinate strictly to make things easy for each other. Here, when A executes the leg sweep, he should draw his left foot toward his body a little to make room for B to leap. After

this he can gyrate heel of left foot sideways and crouches down to sweep back his leg. B should first move his left foot forward at the moment A draws back his left foot a little — to let A draw his foot and to get ready for taking a longer leap.

SECTION TWO

14. B Swings Arm To Deliver Smashing Blow, A Counters With Swing The Hammer Over The Body

Movements:
 1. Placing left foot on floor to left and twisting trunk left halfway, B bends left knee and stretches right foot to form left bow-leg stance. He folds both palms into fists and swings left fist from right armpit in upward-forward curve to smash on A's head (with side of fist). His right fist is held behind body in oblique position (eyes of both fists facing upward). A simultaneously twists trunk right to east, stretches left leg, bends right leg halfway and clenches both palms into fists. As he twists trunk, his right fist is flung on a slant behind body and his left fist is flung horizontally in front of body (front of both fists facing floor). After dodging B's left fist punch, he turns around head to keep eyes on B's left fist (Fig. 33a).
 2. Before end of above movement, B swiftly raises up right fist from behind and flings it forward in curve to smash on A's back with side of fist (fist eye facing upward). His left fist is drawn to side of waist (front of fist facing upward). His eyes on right fist. Meanwhile, A raises left arm with clenched fist and swings it backward in curve to smash down on B's right wrist with that part of forearm close to side of fist (fist eye facing upward). With the momentum of the hand-swing, his trunk twists in leftward-backward direction, and his right fist (fist eye facing upward) is flung up to front in curve. His eyes on his left fist (Fig. 33b).
 3. With above movement still proceeding, A swiftly turns left heel inward, raises up trunk and twists it left, turns right heel outward, bends left knee and straightens right leg to form left bow-leg stance. As he twists trunk, he swings right arm in upward-forward curve to smash on B's head with right fist (fist eye facing upward). He draws left fist (front of fist facing upward) to side of waist. His eyes on his right fist (Fig. 34).

Essentials:

In these moves, both A and B swing their arms to deliver smashing punches. They should keep their shoulders and arms flexible and execute the arm swings with speed. In the execution of the right-arm swing the right foot behind the body should be prevented from shifting sideways.

15. B Parries With Raised Arm, A Does The Ball Kick

Movements:
1. B twists left fist inward and bends elbow to fling left arm to block A's right fist with forearm (fist eye facing floor). At the same time, he draws right fist (fist front facing upward) to side of waist. His eyes on A (Fig. 35).
2. Simultaneously punches toward left fist (fist front) facing floor) to hit at B's breast with knuckles. He simultaneously kicks at B's lower abdomen with right foot (tiptoe pointing forward) and draws right fist to side of waist (fist front facing upward). The moment A executes fist-punch and leg-kick, B shifts left foot backward and straightens it and bends right knee to form right bow-leg stance. Unclenching right fist into palm, he moves right arm in inward — upward direction to block A's left fist with forearm (fingers pointing left, palm front facing forward). He turns left fist into palm which moves downward from front of body to pat on A's right foot (fingers of palm pointing rightward and front of palm facing floor). His eyes on A (Fig. 36).

Essentials:
A's Ball Kick is accompanied by a fist strike. Both the moves should be coordinated, the trunk should be kept perpendicular and the foot firmly planted on the ground. B should do the upward-downward blocking move swiftly and on time; he should keep his shoulders unraised, straighten his back and draw in his waist. The knee must be bent to prevent right heel and left foot from rising up from the floor.

35

36

16. A Executes The Mandarin Duck Feet, B Moves Back To Pat His Leg

Movements:
1. While moving forward with right foot, B turns left fist into palm (front of palm facing upward) and draws it to side of waist (Fig. 37a).

37a

2. With above movement going on, A promptly makes feint frontal kick with left foot, while drawing left fist (fist front facing upward) to side of waist. B simultaneously lifts right foot from ground, ready to retreat backward (Fig. 37b).
3. At moment B lifts up right foot and prepares to retreat, A swiftly lifts up right leg to kick at B's abdomen and lowers left leg to ground. Meanwhile, B springs up on left leg and lowers right foot to ground where left foot used to be; he places left foot on ground behind him, bends right leg and straightens left one to form right bow-leg stance. With front of right palm (fingers pointing forward) he pats on A's right foot. His eyes on his right palm (Fig. 37c).

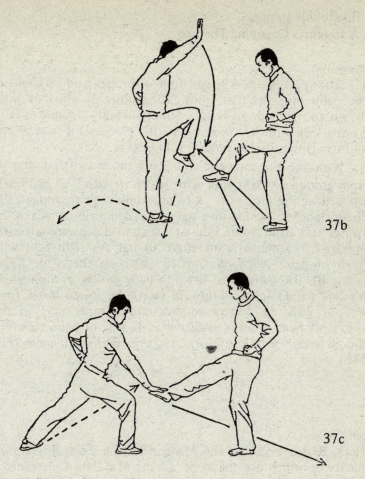

Essentials:
In practice between two persons, The Mandarin Duck Feet is not to be executed as in real combat. In doing the left-foot feint kick, A should just lift up his left leg in front, and his right-foot kick must not touch the other man's body. B's foot-lifting and A's feint kick are to be executed with the same speed. So are his stepping backward and A's lifting up of leg. B's foot-patting move and A's kick are also to be executed with the same speed.

17. B's Double Jumps,
A Executes Chopping The Log.

Movements:
1. After patting on A's right foot with right palm, B clenches the palm into fist (fist front facing upward) which is withdrawn to right side of waist. Simultaneously, he makes feint frontal kick with left foot. A swiftly places right foot behind and straightens it. He bends left knee (Fig. 38a).

2. With above movement still going on, B swiftly jumps up from ground on right foot with which he kicks A's abdomen, while lowering left foot. A twists trunk right to dodge kick. He unclenches left fist into palm and, using elbow as axis, he swings left palm from side of waist in downward-leftward-upward-forward-downward curve to pat A's right foot with front of palm (edge of palm to which attaches little finger facing B). He turns right fist into palm which, at moment of his left palm's leftward-upward swing, begins to move from side of waist in downward-backward-upward curve to rise above his head (fingers pointing at B, side of palm to which thumb attaches facing floor). His eyes on his left palm (Fig. 38b).

Essentials:
Here, B also employs The Mandarin Duck Feet, the requirements of which are the same as The Mandarin Duck Feet A previously executed. In practice exercise, A should not do Chopping The Log as in actual combat by cutting B's shin with his palm. He should execute it just by patting on it so as to prevent injury from being inflicted.

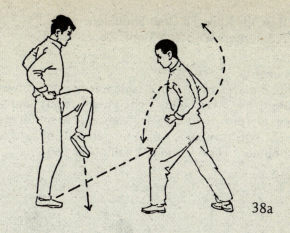

18. B Bends Knee To Grab Shoulder, A Counters With The Monk Ropes The Tiger

Movements:

1. B places right foot beside left one and moves left foot half step back. He bends right knee halfway and straightens left leg to form right bow-leg stance. He simultaneously unfolds right fist into palm which is stretched forward to seize A's left shoulder. His eyes on left palm (Fig. 39).

39

2. A promptly moves right palm down to hold B's right palm and turns trunk left to face west. Meanwhile, he unfolds left palm into fist (fist front facing upward) and flings it leftward by straightening elbow. His eyes on his right palm (Fig. 40a).

40a

3. Before above movement ends, A swiftly swings left fist in downward-backward-upward curve above B's right arm (fist front facing backward). Meanwhile, he twists trunk left to face north and moves right foot to left behind body. His legs cross each other and his eyes on his left fist. The moment A moves his right foot, B steps back with right leg (Fig. 40b).

4. Before end of above movement, A continues to move left foot to left. He bends both knees to form horse-shoe pattern with 50-plus percent of body weight resting on right foot. At same time, he pushes left elbow down to press on B's right wrist. B steps back with left foot, which is stretched against ground, and bends right leg (Fig. 40c).

40b

40c

Essentials:
While executing The Monk Ropes The Tiger in practice exercise by two persons, the elbow should never be pressed down on the opponent's wrist and to be twisted inward and forward as in a real fight. In case the elbow is pressed down, it is not to be done suddenly or pressed against the wrist. Just make the elbow touch with a slight pressure a part of the other man's forearm that is not close to the wrist. Both partners should execute the moves in coordination.

19. B Punches At A's Face, Latter Draws The Bow

Movements:
1. B makes frontal strike at A's forehead with left fist (eye of fist facing upward). His eyes on his left fist (Fig. 41).

41

2. A lets loose right palm's hold on B's right palm and clenches the palm into fist. He raises right forearm to block B's left fist (fist eye facing floor). His eyes on B (Fig. 42a).

3. Before end of above movement, A swiftly thrusts left fist (front of fist facing floor) forward to hit B's abdomen. He shifts weight of body to centre and bends right arm and pulls it rightward. His eyes on his left fist. B simultaneously draws right fist (front of fist facing upward) to side of waist (Fig. 42b).

42a

42b

Essentials:
    In striking out left fist, A should bend right elbow and pull arm rightward — the two moves must be executed with the same speed. In thrusting out fist, B should stop the thrust when the fist gets near A's forehead.

20. B Shuffles Feet To Hammer With Fist, A Does The Bent Phoenix's Elbow

Movements:

1. Withdrawing right foot to place it near inward side of left foot to dodge A's left fist thrust at his breast, B steps forward with left foot. He bends left leg and straightens right leg. He unfolds left fist into palm, which rises up and moves past right side of breast in downward-leftward curve to turn aside B's left fist (Fig. 43a).

43a

2. Before end of above movement, B swiftly swings right fist from side of waist in downward-backward-upward-forward curve to hammer at A's head (fist eye facing upward). At same time, he turns aside A's left fist with left palm which is clenched into fist immediately and drawn to side of waist (front of fist facing upward). His eyes on right fist (Fig. 43b).

43b

3. Swiftly lifting up left fist, A flings left forearm up to block B's right fist (eye of fist facing floor). His eyes on B's right fist (Fig. 44a).

4. Before end of above movement, A twists body left, bends left leg and straightens right one to form left bow-leg stance. Meanwhile, he bends right arm to bring right fist to front of left shoulder (fist touching own body, fist front facing floor). He butts B's below right nipple with elbow. His eyes on his right elbow (Fig. 44b).

Essentials:

In practising The Bent Phoenix's Elbow by two persons, the sharp point of the elbow should only be made to point at B's breast, and not to butt below the nipple. When A makes elbow butt, he should prevent his right foot from shifting sideways. In doing the feet-shuffling move, B's withdrawal of right foot is meant to dodge A's left fist thrust, and the moving forward of his left foot enables him to hammer fist at A. Because of this, B's move in pushing sideways A's left fist with his left palm should be executed the moment he withdraws his right foot. He should move left foot forward and hammer with fist only after warding off A's fist.

44a

44b

21. B Bends Knee To Hold A's Elbow, A Counters With The Monk Strikes The Bell

Movements:
   1. B turns right fist into palm and bending elbow to draw it to spot near face, he moves the palm from front of face to hold the sharp point of A's right elbow (edge of palm to which attaches little finger facing forward). His eyes on his right palm (Fig. 45).

45

   2. A turns left fist into palm and moves it down from above head to seize B's right palm (edge of A's palm to which attaches little finger facing forward) (Fig. 46a).
   3. Before above movement ends, A swiftly raises up from behind left arm right fist which he thrusts in forward curve to strike at B's forehead (front of fist facing upward). He simultaneously stands on left leg and moves right foot forward. His eyes on his right fist (Fig. 46b).

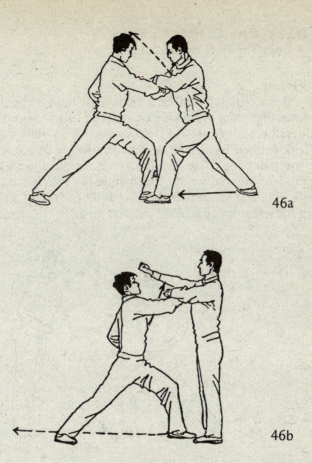

46a

46b

Essentials:
When seizing B's right palm, A should separate thumb from fingers which he uses to grasp that part of B's right palm where thumb and fingers form fork; his thumb should be pressed on side of B's right palm to which attaches little finger. The middle of his palm should be pressed on the back of B's right palm. His drawing of two feet together and his chopping strike on B's head should be executed in coordination and completed at the same time.

22. B Steps Back To Hold A's Elbow, A Does The Deft Needle

Movements:
1. B unfolds left fist into palm with thumb sticking out; he moves the palm from side of waist in forward-upward oblique direction to hold up A's right arm at elbow with front of palm (fork formed by thumb and fingers facing upward). He turns right palm into fist (front of fist facing upward) which he draws to side of waist. Meanwhile, he moves backward with left foot and straightens left leg and bends right one. His eyes on his left palm (Fig. 47).

47

2. A steps forward with right foot and moves left palm (with thumb sticking out) in forward-upward direction to hold up B's left arm at elbow (fork formed by thumb and fingers facing upward). He simultaneously withdraws right fist (fist front facing floor) to side of waist. His eyes on his left palm (Fig. 48a).
3. Before end of above movement, A gyrates right heel sideways and twists trunk left to face south; he bends both knees halfway to form horse-shoe pattern. He thrusts out right fist (fist front facing floor) to hit at B's abdomen with knuckles. He simultaneously twists left forearm inward and bends elbow

to make left palm curve over his head (fingers pointing right, and front of palm facing forward). His eyes on his right fist (Fig. 48b).

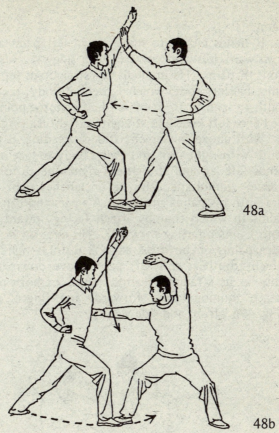

Essentials:
  B's elbow-holding move and drawing back of foot should be completed at the same time. A's elbow-holding and stepping forward should also be completed at the same time. In executing elbow-holding moves, both A and B should not raise up their shoulders. A's elbow-holding, fist-withdrawal, body-twisting and fist-striking moves should be executed with speed and in succession.

23. B Caps A's Ears With Palms, A Does The Monk Strikes The Bell

Movements:
1. B bends elbow to move down left palm and flings it in downward-leftward curve to turn sideways A's right fist with front of palm. He immediately straightens left arm. At same time, his left foot, which is behind body, takes big stride to south to land in front of A's body (tiptoe pointing sideways). He bends left knee and straightens right leg (Fig. 49a).
2. With above movement still proceeding, B takes big stride south with right foot and twists body to face north and A. He bends left leg and straightens right one to form left bow-leg stance. Simultaneously, he unclenches right fist into palm, and both his palms smack on A's ears and cap them (edges of palms to which thumbs attach facing upward, and fingers of both palms pointing forward). His eyes on A. At moment B slaps palms on both his ears, A unfolds right fist into palm which together with left palm move downward from both sides as he straightens arms. (edges of both palms to which attach thumbs facing forward, and fingers pointing floor) (Fig. 49b, front and side views).

49a

49b-front view

49b-side view

3. A raises up both palms and moves them upward between B's arms. He curves both palms near ears to turn sideways A's palms (fingers of A's palms pointing upward). He simultaneously stretches both knees (Fig. 50a).

50a

4. Before above movement ends, A continues to bend knee to lift up left foot, while drawing down both palms (Fig. 50b).

50b

5. With above movement still in progress, A swiftly lowers left foot to ground in front of body, bends left knee and straightens right leg to form left bow-leg stance. Meanwhile, he stretches arms to push both palms toward B's breast (fingers of both palms pointing upward). His eyes on B's breast (Fig. 50c, front and side views).

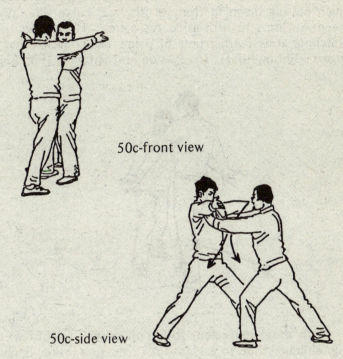

50c-front view

50c-side view

Essentials:
Here B moves his foot from east to north in a curve. B's face faces north from beginning to end. When B moves his left foot obliquely to south, he should gyrate tiptoe sideways. The sideway swing of his left palm should coordinate with his left foot's oblique move, and the ear-capping move of both his palms should be executed in coordination with the big stride taken by his right foot.

24. Both A And B Make Token Steps, And Shield Bodies With Palms

Movements:
1. B, swiftly drawing breast inward when A's on-coming palms are about to touch it, bends both elbows to raise palms, which passing down in front of his face, curve sideways between A's arms to turn aside A's palms. He follows up by stretching arms (with fronts of palms facing each other and fingers pointing floor). His eyes on his right palm (Fig. 51).

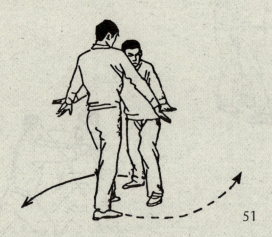

2. With above movement still in progress, B's right foot takes big, oblique stride to east, and A's right foot make big oblique stride to west. Both, bending tiptoes of their right soles inward and twisting bodies left, bend their right legs halfway and shift forward left feet which touch floor with toes in token manner. Simultaneously, both raise their palms and, when their palms reach height a little above their heads, move their left palms forward and hold them paralled to ground (elbows slightly bent). Their right palms are positioned near their left

elbows (fingers of four palms pointing upward, and edges of palms to which attach little fingers facing forward). A and B eye each other (Fig. 52).

52

Essentials:
Fingers of left palm are held higher than eyebrows and those on right palm higher than chin; shoulders are held down loose, back is kept upright with lower abdomen drawn in. Bend both wrists to make palms taut and lower elbows a little. One foot is "real" and other "vague." Left upper sole is straightened taut.

CONCLUDING MOVES

1. **Both A and B stand with feet together and hold fists at sides of waists**

Movements:
 Both A and B simultaneously gyrate right heels inward, straightens their leg and twist trunks forward. A faces south and B north. They draw left feet to side of right feet. Meanwhile, they clenches palms into fists and draw them to sides of waists (fronts of palms facing floor). Their eyes on each other (Fig. 53).

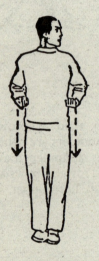 

53

2. A and B stand at attention to wind up practice exercise.

Movements:
   Both A and B unclench fists into palms and lower them to sides of hips, turn faces right and stand at attention. (Fig. 54).

54

Essentials:
   As this is a winding up move, the head should be held upright, chin drawn in and eyes looking straight forward. Chest should be held up, back straightened, lower abdomen drawn in and arms lowered naturally to sides. One should be in high spirits and breathes calmly.